SPORTS HEROES

EVAN LONGORIA

Sloan MacRae

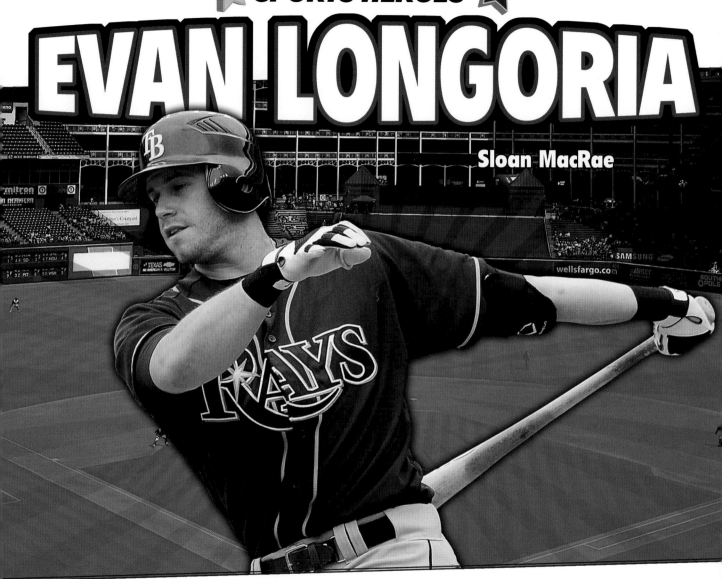

PowerKiDS
press™

New York

Published in 2012 by The Rosen Publishing Group, Inc.
29 East 21st Street, New York, NY 10010

First Edition

Editor: Jennifer Way
Book Design: Julio Gil

Photo Credits: Cover, p. 5 Mark Cunningham/MLB Photos via Getty Images; cover (background) Ronald Martinez/Getty Images; p. 4 Mitchell Layton/Getty Images; p. 6 J. Meric/Getty Images; pp. 7, 21 Jeff Gross/Getty Images; pp. 8–9 Gary Bogdon/Sports Illustrated/Getty Images; pp. 10, 11, 12, 13 (left, right) Reuben Canales/WireImage/Getty Images; pp. 14, 15, 18–19 Rich Pilling/MLB Photos via Getty Images; p. 16 Jim McIsaac/Getty Images; p. 17 Jed Jacobsohn/Getty Images; p. 20 Jason Merritt/Getty Images for Pepsi MLB Refresh Project; p. 22 Nick Laham/Getty Images.

Library of Congress Cataloging-in-Publication Data

MacRae, Sloan.
  Evan Longoria / by Sloan MacRae. — 1st ed.
     p. cm. — (Sports heroes)
  Includes index.
  ISBN 978-1-4488-6163-7 (library binding) — ISBN 978-1-4488-6284-9 (pbk.) —
ISBN 978-1-4488-6285-6 (6-pack)
  1. Longoria, Evan, 1985-–Juvenile literature. 2. Baseball players—United States—Biography—Juvenile literature. I. Title.
  GV865.L665M33 2012
  796.357092—dc23
  [B]
                                    2011023997

Manufactured in the United States of America

CPSIA Compliance Information: Batch #WW12PK: For Further Information contact Rosen Publishing, New York, New York at 1-800-237-9932

CONTENTS

A FAST-RISING STAR

There are very few superstars in sports. One reason for this is that it often takes **athletes** several years to become great players. It did not take several years for Evan Longoria to become one. It took only several weeks in **Major League Baseball** (MLB) before he became known as one of the most exciting hitters.

A power hitter like Longoria tends to hit the ball hard and far. This kind of hitting can give teammates who are already on base a chance to score runs. »»

Longoria is a **third baseman** for the Tampa Bay Rays. He is one of the best power hitters in the game, but he is also great with his glove. Longoria loves turning **double plays** from third base. Because he became so good so quickly, there is no telling how many records Longoria might break.

«« When Longoria makes a double play, that means he has gotten two players from the other team out.

PLAYING WATER POLO

Evan was born on October 7, 1985, in Downey, California. Sports were very important to the Longoria family. By the time he was in high school, Evan was playing baseball and water polo. Water polo is like basketball, but it is played in a swimming pool. It is a difficult game to play because it requires you to be

Many professional baseball players played a second sport in high school. Football, basketball, and soccer are more common second sports than water polo. Longoria has said that the sport helped his endurance and his all-around fitness.

a strong swimmer. The game changes quickly because the ball moves from one side of the pool to the other.

Playing water polo helped make Evan a good athlete. Fortunately for the baseball world, Evan decided to quit water polo so he could spend more time playing baseball.

Evan played water polo for two years on his high-school team before he decided he wanted to focus on baseball. Here he is playing for the Rays in 2010.

TOO SMALL FOR THE GAME

Evan played baseball all four years at St. John Bosco High School in Bellflower, California. By his senior, or final, year, he was one of the best young ballplayers in California. He was also one of the smallest. Most college **scouts** did not consider him for the best college teams.

Evan worked hard to become stronger, but he also had to be patient because he was still growing at the end of high school. He did not reach his full height of 6 feet 2 inches (1.9 m) until he was in college.

Evan lifted weights and worked out hard to become bigger, but it was no use. He was still too small. None of the big baseball colleges gave him a chance. Evan did not give up. He knew he could be a **professional** baseball player. In a few short years, many people would feel foolish for counting Evan Longoria out.

⭐ BIGGER AT RIO HONDO

Because no major schools were interested in him, Longoria had to play baseball for a **junior college**. In 2003, Longoria entered Rio Hondo Community College as a freshman, or first-year student.

Longoria proved very quickly that he was the best player on the team. He was

Rio Hondo Community College was near Longoria's hometown of Downey, California. Here he is in 2006, after he transferred to Long Beach State. »»

also still growing. Longoria grew 2 inches (5 cm) in his freshman year at Rio Hondo. He was taller and stronger, and he could hit the ball very far. His **batting average** after his first Rio Hondo season was .430. A .280 batting average is very good. A .300 is amazing. Longoria's .430 was out of this world!

««« Here is Longoria playing for Long Beach State against the University of California–Irvine in 2006.

⭐ LONG BEACH STATE

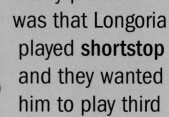

After Longoria's freshman year at Rio Hondo, the big schools noticed him. In 2004, Long Beach State offered him a **scholarship** to transfer for his sophomore, or second, year. The only problem was that Longoria played **shortstop** and they wanted him to play third base. Third basemen have to throw a long way. They must have powerful arms.

Longoria has said that he sometimes had a tough time ≫ during his first year playing third base at Long Beach. Once he got used to it, playing that position became easier for him.

Here is Longoria batting for Long Beach State in 2006.

Longoria had a .320 average in his first season and led his new team in **stolen bases**. In his second year at Long Beach, he batted .353. He was now one of the best young players in the game.

Longoria had a great batting average at Long Beach. Here he has hit a home run against the University of the Pacific. >>>

⭐ IN THE MINOR LEAGUES

The road to the major league is a long one. Players must learn how to hit faster pitches and how to play with the very best. The Tampa Bay Rays picked Longoria to play for them in 2006, but he was not quite ready for the majors. Tampa sent him to play for their **minor-league** teams.

The All-Star Futures Game is a minor-league baseball all-star game. It is played the same week as the MLB All-Star Game. Here is Longoria during the 2007 All-Star Futures Game.

He did not stay in the minors for long. By 2008, the Rays believed Longoria was ready. They were right. He batted in a run in his very first game. A few days later, he hit his first major-league home run against the New York Yankees, one of the best teams in baseball.

In 2006 and 2007, Longoria played for several of the Rays' minor-league teams. They were the Hudson Valley Renegades, the Visalia Oaks, the Montgomery Biscuits, and the Durham Bulls. Here is Longoria during the 2007 All-Star Futures Game.

★ ROOKIE OF THE YEAR

New players are called rookies. Longoria became one of the best rookies of all time. Pitchers from other teams hated to play the Rays because they had to face him. Longoria was named an all-star in his first season. This means he got to play in the All-Star Game. This is a special game in which fans

Longoria's batting average ▶▶▶ was .272 during his first year with the Rays.

and baseball **experts** get to pick the two teams by voting for the very best players. Most players never get to be all-stars.

Longoria also helped the Rays make it to the **postseason** for the very first time. Thanks to him, the Rays even got to play in the 2008 **World Series**. Longoria was voted 2008's Rookie of the Year.

◀◀◀ In 2008, the Rays made it to the World Series for the first time. They ended up losing the series to the Philadelphia Phillies, though. Here is Longoria catching a pop fly during Game 5 of the series.

⭐ GOLD GLOVES

Longoria received every vote when he was named Rookie of the Year. Nobody else stood a chance! This had happened to only five other Rookies of the Year. Longoria was not finished winning awards.

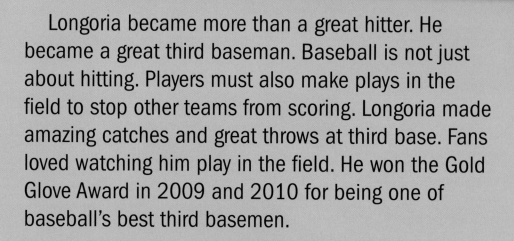

Longoria played on the American League All-Star team in 2008, 2009, and 2010. Here he is watching the 2008 All-Star Game from the dugout. »»

Longoria became more than a great hitter. He became a great third baseman. Baseball is not just about hitting. Players must also make plays in the field to stop other teams from scoring. Longoria made amazing catches and great throws at third base. Fans loved watching him play in the field. He won the Gold Glove Award in 2009 and 2010 for being one of baseball's best third basemen.

⭐ OFF THE FIELD

Longoria believes in helping his community. To do this, he works with many **charities** in both his new town of Tampa, Florida, and in his home state of California. In 2011, Longoria held yoga classes to raise money for the Moffitt Cancer Center, in Tampa. This raised thousands of dollars for the hospital.

Longoria likes playing all kinds of sports. ⟫⟫
Here he is playing golf at the 2011 Bob
Hope Classic in La Quinta, California. This is
a golf tournament in which both professional
golfers and celebrities take part.

Some people think Evan is related to a famous actress named Eva Longoria. They think Evan and Eva are brother and sister because they have almost the same name. They are not related, but Eva did send Evan a good-luck gift for his first All-Star Game and thanked him for "doing the Longoria name proud."

⟪⟪ Longoria (top row, second from
right) and other MLB players are
seen here painting a mural at a
community center in Anaheim,
California, in 2010.

21

It took Longoria only 135 games to help the Rays score 100 runs.

Longoria loves to play the video game *Guitar Hero* with other Tampa Bay Rays players.

A famous video shows Longoria making an amazing catch. This was a viral video he did as an advertisement for Gillette razors.

Sometimes fans of other teams call out the name "Eva" so that Evan will not play well. This does not often work.

Evan Longoria and Eva Longoria have one thing in common. Their families are both of Mexican-American descent.

Longoria became the sixth rookie in baseball history to have a hit in both the All-Star Game and the World Series.

Longoria studied criminology at Long Beach State. This is an important subject for police.

The Rays play the song "Down and Out" when Longoria comes up to bat.

Longoria both bats and throws right-handed.

Longoria set a record by hitting six postseason home runs in his rookie season.

GLOSSARY

athletes (ATH-leets) People who take part in sports.

batting average (BA-ting A-veh-rij) A number that measures how good a hitter is. It is the number of hits divided by at bats.

charities (CHER-uh-teez) Groups that give help to the needy.

double plays (DUH-bul PLAYZ) Plays in baseball in which two players are out.

experts (EK-sperts) People who know a lot about a subject.

junior college (JOON-yer KAH-lij) A two-year school that a student may attend after high school.

Major League Baseball (MAY-jur LEEG BAYS-bawl) The top group of baseball teams in the United States.

minor-league (my-nur-LEEG) A group of teams on which players play before they are good enough for the next level.

postseason (pohst-SEE-zun) Games played after the regular season.

professional (pruh-FESH-nul) Someone who is paid for what he or she does.

scholarship (SKAH-lur-ship) Money given to someone to pay for school.

scouts (SKOWTS) People who help sports teams find new, young players.

shortstop (SHORT-stop) The baseball player who stands between second and third base.

stolen bases (STOHL-en BAYS-ez) When base runners successfully make it to the next base while the pitcher is throwing the ball to home plate.

third baseman (THURD BAYS-mun) The player whose job it is to defend the area around third base.

World Series (WURLD SEER-eez) A group of games in which the two best baseball teams play against each other.

INDEX

A
All-Star Game, 16, 21, 22
athlete(s), 4, 7

B
ball, 7, 11
baseball, 4, 6–8, 10, 15, 18
batting average, 11, 13

C
California, 6, 8, 20
catch(es), 18, 22
chance, 8, 18
colleges, 8, 10

F
fans, 16, 18, 22

H
high school, 6, 8
hitter(s), 4–5, 18
home run(s), 15, 22

P
player(s), 4, 8, 10, 13–14, 16–18, 22
postseason, 17

R
record(s), 5, 22
run(s), 15, 22

S
school(s), 6, 8, 10, 12
season, 11, 13, 16, 22
sports, 4, 6

T
Tampa, Florida, 20
Tampa Bay Rays, 5, 14–17, 22
team(s), 8, 10, 13–18, 22
third base, 5, 12, 18
third baseman, 5, 12, 18
throws, 18

V
vote, 18

W
weights, 8
World Series, 17, 22

Y
yoga classes, 20

WEB SITES

Due to the changing nature of Internet links, PowerKids Press has developed an online list of Web sites related to the subject of this book. This site is updated regularly. Please use this link to access the list:
www.powerkidslinks.com/hero/longoria/